J
6.088
W8r

World Book's Learning Ladders

World of Pets

WORLD BOOK

a Scott Fetzer company
Chicago

www.worldbookonline.com

WORLD BOOK

233 N. Michigan Avenue
Chicago, IL 60601
U.S.A.

For information about other World Book publications, visit our Web site at
http://www.worldbookonline.com or call 1-800-WORLDBK (967-5325).

For information about sales to schools and libraries, call 1-800-975-3250 (United States);
1-800-837-5365 (Canada).

Library of Congress Cataloging-in-Publication Data

World of pets.
    p. cm. -- (World Book's learning ladders)
  Summary: "Introduction to common household pets
using simple text, illustrations, and photos. Features
include puzzles and games, fun facts, a resource list,
and an index"-- Provided by publisher.
  Includes index.
  ISBN 978-0-7166-7745-1
  1. Pets--Juvenile literature. I. World Book, Inc.
SF416.2.W67 2011
636.088'7--dc22
                                        2010022380

World Book's Learning Ladders
Set 2 ISBN: 978-0-7166-7746-8

Printed in China by Shenzhen Wing King Tong Paper Products Co., Ltd.
Shenzhen, Guangdong
1st printing December 2010

Editorial
  Editor in Chief: Paul A. Kobasa
  Associate Manager, Supplementary Publications:
    Cassie Mayer
  Writer: Shawn Brennan
  Editor: Brian Johnson
  Researcher: Cheryl Graham
  Manager, Contracts & Compliance
  (Rights & Permissions): Loranne K. Shields

Graphics and Design
  Manager: Tom Evans
  Coordinator, Design Development and Production:
    Brenda B. Tropinski
  Photographs Editor: Kathy Creech

Pre-Press and Manufacturing
  Director: Carma Fazio
  Manufacturing Manager: Steven Hueppchen
  Production/Technology Manager: Anne Fritzinger

Photographic credits: Cover: © Jack Z.Young, Shutterstock; WORLD BOOK illustration by Q2A
Media; Shutterstock; p4: Ardea London; p5, p6, p9, p11, p26, p27, p30: Shutterstock; p8, p12,
p16, p18: Alamy Images; p10: Getty Images; p20: Masterfile; p22: Dreamstime

Illustrators: WORLD BOOK illustration by Q2A Media; WORLD BOOK illustration by Walter
Linsenmaier; WORLD BOOK illustration by Colin Newman; WORLD BOOK illustration by
Michael Hampshire and Jettie Griffin

What's inside?

This book looks at some popular types of pets to help you decide which pet is right for you. You will also learn about what you need to do to keep your pet healthy and happy.

Choosing a pet

Pets are animals that keep us company. Pets can be playful and loyal friends. But taking care of a pet is a big job. Pets depend on us to feed them and keep them clean. They also depend on us to take care of their health. The pets shown in the big picture are gerbils *(JUR buhls)*. Read on to see which pet is right for you!

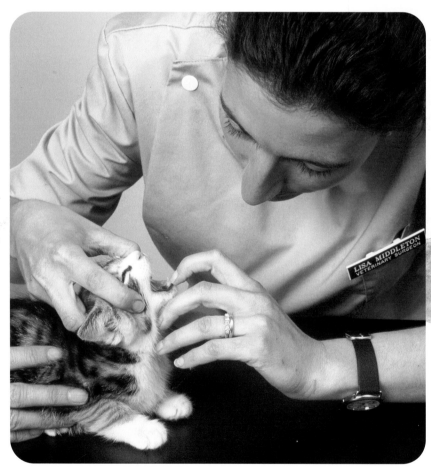

An animal doctor called a veterinarian *(VEHT uhr uh NEHR ee uhn)* checks a pet to make sure it is healthy. If a pet gets hurt or sick, it should be taken to a vet.

Pets should always have fresh **water** to drink.

A small animal should be kept in a **cage** that is big enough for it to move around a lot.

It's a fact!
Some of the United States presidents had unusual pets: a wallaby, hyena, badger, herd of elephants, and an alligator!

Many types of pets are happier and healthier when they can **exercise**.

Pets need proper **food** to stay healthy.

Bedding helps keep a pet clean and dry. The bedding must be changed when it gets dirty.

 # Dog

Dogs were the first animals tamed by people. Thousands of years ago, people used them as watchdogs. Over time, people trained dogs to help hunt wild animals and to herd sheep and cattle. Today, many people keep dogs as pets. Dogs are loyal and friendly companions. But they need lots of love and attention. The big picture shows a German shepherd dog.

A wet **nose** is often the sign of a healthy dog.

There are many different breeds, or kinds, of dogs. The smallest breed of dog is the chihuahua *(chee WAH wah)*. The Great Dane is one of the largest of all dogs.

A dog can **hear** sounds too high for human ears to hear.

It's a fact!

Scientists believe that all of the dogs we know today are related to wolves—even though some dogs no longer look anything like wolves!

Your dog should wear a **collar** with tags. This will help you find your pet if it gets lost.

A dog wags its **tail** when it is happy or excited.

A dog **pants** to cool off.

Long-haired dogs need **grooming** often. Brushing gets fleas and ticks out of a dog's fur.

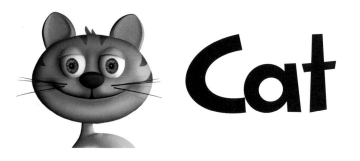

Cat

Cats are graceful and clever animals that enjoy doing things for themselves. They can also be playful and curious. Unlike dogs, most cats cannot be trained to come or fetch. But they are good indoor pets because they can easily learn how to use a litter box. And they do not need to be groomed often because they clean themselves every day!

A cat rubs against us to mark us with its scent.

Padded **paws** hide a cat's sharp claws.

A cat has a rough **tongue** that can pick up dirt and fleas and comb its fur.

Whiskers are good for feeling things in the dark.

A cat's **eyes** are good at seeing movement.

Cats love to play with **toys**.

Rabbit

Rabbits are cute, curious creatures that like to explore the world around them. Rabbits can be kept indoors or outdoors in a type of cage called a hutch. Pet rabbits may be black, brown, gray, white, or even spotted. They may live as long as 10 to 15 years.

A mother rabbit may have as many as 12 babies at a time, and she may give birth several times a year. Baby rabbits are called kits.

Rabbits move their long **ears** together or one at a time to catch sounds from every direction.

It's a fact!

A rabbit's teeth never stop growing! Rabbits wear down their teeth by moving their jaw from side to side when they chew plants.

Rabbits have soft **fur**.

Rabbits use their powerful **back legs** to hop or stand upright.

Bird

Birds can make good pets for people who live in small homes or apartments. They live in cages that take up little space. People like pet birds for their singing, beauty, and playfulness. Parakeets are one of the most popular pet birds. They can learn to talk and perform tricks. The big picture shows a kind of parakeet called a budgerigar *(buhj uhr ee GAHR)*, or budgie.

A cockatoo is a kind of parrot that has a crest of feathers that it can raise and lower. Cockatoos make fun pets because they can do tricks.

A budgie's cage should have plenty of **toys**.

A budgie has brightly colored **feathers**.

A budgie's strong **beak** cracks seeds to eat.

A budgie's **toes** help the bird hold onto a perch and climb.

13

Going for a walk

When you take your dog for a walk, you may meet other animals along the way. Will your dog make a friend or see an enemy?

14

Words you know

Here are some words that you learned earlier. Say them out loud, then try to find the things in the picture.

feathers   paws   collar

fur   tail   beak

How are the dogs greeting each other?

How many birds do you see?

15

Guinea pig

Many people keep guinea (*GIHN ee*) pigs as pets. Guinea pigs are not really pigs. They are rodents, like rats and squirrels. Pet guinea pigs may be white, black, brown, red, or a mixture of colors. Pet guinea pigs need a cage with plenty of air and fresh drinking water. They eat dry grains, greens, and hay.

In some countries, guinea pigs are popular as show animals.

Guinea pigs drink out of a **water bottle**.

Guinea pigs like to hide in a **shelter** during the day.

Guinea pigs use their sharp front **teeth** for gnawing plants.

It's a fact!

Guinea pigs are not related to pigs. They belong to a group of rodents called cavies. No one is sure how guinea pigs got their name!

A healthy guinea pig has shiny **eyes**.

Guinea pigs have small **ears**.

Sharp **claws** are good for digging.

Hamster

Hamsters are popular pets because they are cute and fairly easy to care for. Like guinea pigs, hamsters are rodents. Many kinds of hamsters like to live alone. They should not be kept in a cage with other hamsters.

A hamster's **cage** should be kept in an area free of cold air.

Dwarf hamsters are smaller hamsters with furry feet. Unlike most hamsters, they like to live in pairs.

Hamsters carry food in their large **cheek pouches.**............

Hamsters dig .... **burrows** for nesting, food storage, and body wastes.

It's a
fact!

Pet hamsters can give birth as often as once a month!

Hamsters often run on an **exercise wheel** at night.

19

Hermit crab

Hermit crabs live in the empty shells of snails or other animals. When the crab grows larger, it finds a bigger shell in which to live. Hermit crabs will eat just about anything. But they need a balanced diet and fresh water. They also need a moist, warm environment. A plastic or glass aquarium with sand makes a good "crabitat"!

Hermit crabs like to climb and play on rocks and **driftwood**.

The coconut crab is the largest land hermit crab. It feeds on the meat of coconuts. An adult coconut crab grows its own shell.

A **wet sponge** helps keep moisture in the air.

Give your hermit crab a variety of **shells** to grow into.

It's a fact!

The hermit crab doesn't live up to its name. People who are hermits live alone. But hermit crabs like company and live in groups!

Lighting helps keep the tank warm. Use a **thermometer** to check the temperature of the tank.

Water should always be available for your hermit crab to drink.

80°F

The hermit crab drinks and feeds itself with its small right **pincher.** It uses its large left pincher to move around and defend itself.

Fish

Many people enjoy watching their pet fish swim about. Fish usually need less attention than other pets. But they do need just the right living environment. The big picture shows a Betta, or Siamese fightingfish. Bettas cannot live together because they will fight one another!

It's a fact!
The oldest known goldfish have lived more than 40 years!

An **aquarium** should be big enough for the fish to swim about. An adult should clean it regularly.

Plants help supply oxygen for fish.

The Betta swims with its long, waving **fins and tail**.

A guppy is a small tropical fish that is a popular aquarium pet. Guppies give birth to live young. Most other fish lay eggs.

Be sure to feed your fish only the amount of **food** it needs.

A fish's slippery skin is covered with **scales**.

Ask your pet store owner what **equipment** your aquarium needs to keep your fish healthy.

At the pet shop

You can buy food and other supplies at a pet shop. You may even find a new friend to bring home! Look at all the different kinds of animals. Which pet is right for you?

24

Words you know

Here are some words that you learned earlier. Say them out loud, then try to find the things in the picture.

pincher   exercise wheel   cage

water bottle   aquarium

What kind of animal is the boy pointing at?

Did you know?

A cat may spend up to 16 hours a day sleeping. Older cats sleep even more!

The largest goldfish can weigh 6 ½ pounds (3 kilograms) or more!

6.5 lbs
3 kg

Hellooo

Cockatoos are some of the noisiest parrots! Wild cockatoos use their loud voices to communicate with one another across long distances in forests.

Guppies have babies as often as every four to six weeks!

Dogs have lived with people for at least 14,000 years—longer than any other animal!

In 1954, a Japanese laboratory sent 22 gerbils to the United States for use in scientific research. These animals became the ancestors of pet gerbils in the United States.

Puzzles

Close-up!

We've zoomed in on the body parts of some pets. Can you figure out which pets you are looking at?

1

2

3

Answers on page 32.

Take me home!

Can you match each pet to its home? Follow the lines to find out!

fish rabbit bird

cage aquarium hutch

28

Who's alike?

1 Which five pets have fur?

2 Which two pets are rodents?

3 Which six pets need cages or aquariums?

bird

cat

dog

hamster

rabbit

fish

hermit crab

guinea pig

Answers on page 32.

True or false

Can you figure out which of these statements are true? Turn to the page numbers given to help you find the answers.

3 Scientists believe that all dogs are related to wolves. **Go to page 7.**

1 A hermit crab doesn't like company. **Go to page 21.**

4 A goldfish can live to 100 years. **Go to page 22.**

2 The guinea pig is related to pigs. **Go to page 17.**

5 Cats do not often land on their feet. **Go to page 9.**

Answers on page 32.

Find out more

Books

Peculiar Pets by Teresa Domnauer (School Specialty Publishing, 2007)
Many unusual animals are kept as pets around the world. Read this book to learn about them.

Pet Science: 50 Purr-fectly Woof-worthy Activities for You and Your Pets by Veronika A. Gunther, Rain Newcomb, and Tom LaBaff (Lark Books, 2006)
What makes your pet howl, yowl, and meow? Why do cats see so well in the dark? This book includes a collection of activities that teach all about family pets.

Please Don't Tease Tootsy by Margaret Chamberlain (Dutton Children's Books, 2008)
In this story about caring for furry friends, you'll receive helpful hints on how not to treat your pet.

Top Pets for Kids with American Humane (Enslow Publishers, 2009). Six volumes: *Top 10 Birds for Kids* by Wendy Mead, *Top 10 Cats for Kids* by Dana Meachen Rau, *Top 10 Dogs for Kids* by Ann Gaines, *Top 10 Fish for Kids* by Dana Meachen Rau, *Top 10 Reptiles and Amphibians for Kids* by Ann Gaines, *Top 10 Small Mammals for Kids* by Ann Gaines. These books can help you pick the best pet for you and your family. The top 10 animals listed in each book are approved by the American Humane Association.

Web sites

HealthyPet.com
http://www.healthypet.com/KidsKlub/Default.aspx
The Kids Klub offers activities, fun facts, and guidelines for young pet owners.

It's My Life: Pets
http://pbskids.org/itsmylife/family/pets/index.html
Includes such topics as choosing and finding the right pet, getting permission to have a pet, and caring for a pet.

Petpourrie
http://www.avma.org/careforanimals/kidscorner/default.asp
The American Veterinary Medical Association suggests activities that will help children learn about caring for a pet.

U.S. Presidential Pets: Then and Now
http://kids.nationalgeographic.com/kids/stories/animalsnature/uspresidentialpets/
Fun facts and stories about the pets owned by our presidents, from the National Geographic Kids Web site.

Answers

Puzzles
from pages 28 and 29

Close-up!
1. bird
2. guinea pig
3. fish

Who's alike?
1. cat, dog, guinea pig, hamster, rabbit
2. guinea pig, hamster
3. bird, fish, guinea pig, hamster, hermit crab, rabbit

True or false
from page 30

1. false
2. false
3. true
4. false
5. false

Index